Jesus, My Higher Power

Rosemary

ISBN 978-0-9972085-1-1 (paperback)
ISBN 978-0-9972085-0-4 (ebook)

Published by AquaZebra, www.AquaZebra.com

AquaZebra™
Book Publishing

Author: Rosemary

Book Designer Mark E. Anderson, AquaZebra

AquaZebra™
Web, Book & Print Design

www.AquaZebra.com

Introduction and Dedication

This book is dedicated to Jesus, my Lord, Savior and Higher Power. We look to Him for victory because victory is in Jesus. Why is my hope in Jesus? Why is Jesus my Higher Power? Let us learn of Him. Let us increase in knowledge and wisdom. Let us receive His great love, power, peace, and joy. Let us know the truth which sets us free. We accept our new life in Christ, and we give praise and thanks to God.

If God is a Spirit, and He is incarnated in Jesus Christ, His Son, and if Jesus Christ, after his death and resurrection, sent His Holy Spirit to dwell in us, then we are spiritually one in Jesus Christ, the Son, and one with God, the Father.

If God is Love, then this spirit of unity or oneness is also one of Love. Our spiritual experience makes real to us that in the spiritual realm we can be one with God, Jesus and the Holy Spirit. We can dwell in this great spiritual Love, Peace and Power.

We dwell in this spiritual unity, given to us, when we love and accept God, His Son, Jesus Christ, and His Holy Spirit. God's great Love, Peace, Power and Grace will do for us those things we are unable to do for ourselves.

Jesus, My Higher Power

Why Is Jesus My Higher Power?

Many people in 12 step fellowships may ask the question to a believer in Jesus Christ, "Why is Jesus your Higher Power?" As we know, we in 12 step fellowships look to a Higher Power or to God as we understand Him. It is my intent to simply answer the above question of "Why is Jesus My Higher Power?" to those who may ask it.

It is in understanding God's love that we are set free. God's love is powerful, redeeming, and eternal. He never changes. Through learning about Jesus Christ, God's Son, we grow in understanding of God and His great power. We become aware that the same power that raised Jesus from the dead is the same power available to us. We just need to admit we need help, seek Him, come to believe, and surrender our limited power, will, and lives to Him. It is then we realize that we are not alone in our difficulties but have supernatural help.

Having studied the scriptures about Jesus, we learn of His great power. In addition, we can experience a spiritual connection with Him, showing us a vaster realm of reality that most of us are unaware of. Jesus not only came to earth to live an earthly life but He also dwells out of the realm of space and time.

Examples of His power over this material world can be found in many biblical accounts. He healed the sick, raised the dead, cast out demons, walked on water, multiplied food, turned water to wine, and rose from the dead. There is a scripture that says "I can do all things through Christ who strengthens me." It is apparent to me that, on my own, I am powerless, but through my Higher Power, Jesus Christ, I can do all things. I believe there is a spiritual connection, a spiritual unity that unites my spirit with a Higher Power. Jesus said He and His Father are one, and we can be one with Him and His Father. It is in this Unity that we overcome and are victorious.

Jesus has said He has all authority in Heaven and Earth as both a mortal man and as the divine Son of God. He also lives now. As a spiritual Being, He dwells both inside and outside the realm of space and time, and through His Holy Spirit indwells all of life, all who believe. He said that He is the way, the truth, and the life. In Jesus is life, is power beyond what our mere mortal brains can comprehend. When we connect our mortal mind to his Mind, to his Power, we receive supernatural help. When we stay connected to the

Mind of Christ, we live in harmony and in unity with Him and others. We dwell in Love, in Beauty, and in Truth. He is able to do for us what we cannot do for ourselves. All He asks us is to have faith, not to doubt, to trust Him and to keep His commandments. It is true that, in His presence, there is no pain - just complete peace and joy.

There is a vastly greater realm where there is no pain. That realm is very near to us at all times. We are to lay aside the weight that so easily besets us. That is, we should not carry around any heavy burden that only weighs us down and keeps us less effective, less joyful. In God's presence is fullness of joy, and the joy of the Lord is our strength. So let us cast our cares upon Him. He asks us to. We can then be free to live life fully and to enjoy it. Then, we are better able to have more energy and enthusiasm to spread the Gospel and to live the abundant life. We praise God and rejoice in Him. We are glad for each day and choose a heart of cheer and hope. We are not in denial to the sufferings, sadness, and tribulations of life nor to the temptations and evils, but we know that through Jesus Christ we have overcome. He is the Alpha and the Omega. If we believe in Him, we will never die but have eternal life. This is a spiritual life of good, peace, love, truth, righteousness, joy, beauty, and power. It is a life that will know no pain, disease, evil, nor death.

Many of our addictions or dependencies are caused by a fear of being alone, an emptiness or void inside a lonely hole in the soul. This can only be filled by God's spirit. Once we receive His spirit, we lose the need to fill ourselves with unhealthy dependencies. Our soul, which had been in a prison, is set free to live and enjoy life abundantly.

We need to turn to Jesus, our Higher Power. He will completely heal the broken areas, remove our defects of character, reconcile us to God and to ourselves and bring us home to Him and to ourselves. We need to have Him restore the broken years, to renew our joy and childlike happiness. His atonement cleanses us from all sin, and we are born again - new and fresh. We see the world through new glasses. We live our life by spiritual principles. We are thankful for God's grace.

Jesus is the Light of the World. When we follow Jesus, we are living in the Light. Our focus is on the Light first and foremost and not on other people or circumstances. We are able to release unhealthy attachments that hold us down. We detach from worldly concerns, catastrophic fears, harmful people, and focus on a relationship with God, Jesus, and His Holy Spirit. This relationship is full of peace and beauty, love and power.

Jesus is indeed the Savior of the world. Let Him be the power people turn to. We must remove ourselves from the crutches we lean on. We need to let go of the reins of control, thoughts, obsessions over others behavior problems and give them to God.

We need to stand fast with trust in the Lord and have faith in Him. God is Sovereign, and in His world all things prosper. We have faith; He has the power. Ask only for His will. Let us be firm and steadfast and not compromise with evil. Let us learn not to condone nor enable unrighteousness.

Let us daily seek God's will.

Growing spiritually is also growing in self-love and self-esteem. It is realizing our value and worth through Christ and placing a higher sense of value on ourselves. Our life is in Christ. We have broken out of the victim patterns, because in Christ we are victorious. We are committed to our Higher Power and His will for our lives.

What Jesus Will Show You

Jesus showed me I am not alone. He showed me unconditional love and acceptance. He forgave me and showed me how to forgive. Jesus displayed that there is life after life. Jesus fills the void, the emptiness, in one's life. His intimate relationship with us gives us spiritual union and connectedness, instead of isolation. He offers hope when we despair. He unites us into one with Him, His Father and others. He gives us a positive focus. He tells us how important our beliefs and faith are, how important our thoughts are. He renews our mind.

We need to try to take loving, gentle, good care of ourselves and give ourselves the nurturing we would give a little child. We need to make choices that are in our best interest that are also beneficial for the common good. We look to God daily for His love, strength, courage, and hope. We try to grow in purity, love and joy of the Lord. We try to maintain a peaceful mind and heart and remove ourselves from situations or people when we lose our serenity.

We give thanks to God and praise Him for our lives, for He is faithful to keep His promises for peace and to restore the broken areas of our lives. He says "I will restore the years the locust have eaten." Remember, He is the Great I Am, the Alpha and the Omega who dwells beyond our limited view of space and time. With Him all things are possible.

What Can Jesus Do for You?

He shows you His great love. He forgives your sins. He carries your burdens. He heals you. He delivers you from unhealthy dependencies and afflictions. He can take away your need to depend on chemicals. He reveals His love, beauty, power, peace, glory and closeness to you. He gives you worth and value. He raises your self-esteem. He gives you a proper self-concept and identity as a beloved child of God. He gives you gentleness and compassion for yourself and others. He increases your wisdom of what is righteous behavior. He breaks your obsessions or compulsions. He gives you His peace. He gives you eternal life.

Who Is Jesus? He Is the Son of God.

What can he do for you? He can save you, heal you, give you life after death, fill you with His great love. Why do you need Jesus? How can you develop a relationship with Him? When will you see Jesus? Where is Jesus? Jesus is here. He, His Father God and the Holy Spirit are omnipresent. What is the role of Jesus? Jesus came to save us, to show us God's love, power and victory over disease and death. Why is Jesus significant? He gives hope and help, and reveals to us a higher reality and power. When will Jesus reveal more of Himself? He reveals Himself beyond mortality. He is evidenced by transformed lives. How does Jesus reveal Himself? He reveals Himself through His Holy Spirit, His love, peace, power, through healings, changed lives, deliverance, His touch, His compassion, His comfort and through His word the Holy Scriptures. He also reveals His love through other believers. How does Jesus help me? He shows me that I'm not alone. He tells me that I am loved and forgiven. He reveals that there is a realm of greater beauty, peace, love, power, and truth with Him, where there is no pain. He says that I must have faith, obey, trust, and believe. He says that I must not doubt nor sin. There is great glory in His presence. Just ask

Him to be your Savior and surrender your life to Him. He is faithful and just. He will be your Higher Power.

Why Is our Hope in Jesus?

Jesus heals the sick. He has victory over disease. Jesus cast out demons or evil spirits. Jesus raises the dead. In Him is eternal life. Jesus forgives our sins. Jesus took the penalty for our sins on the cross. He redeemed us. Jesus loves us. Jesus has power over nature. He walks on water, calms the storm, multiples food to feed the crowd. Jesus rose from the dead. Jesus promised to send His Holy Spirit. Jesus promised to help us achieve a new life in His kingdom where there is no disease, sin or sadness. Jesus promised to return. Jesus had eyewitnesses who testified and died for the gospel truth. We give Him our thanks and praise. Jesus is the Savior of this earth.

Jesus is drawing us closer to Him. God wants to be first in our lives. Our codependent behaviors interfere at times with our spiritual growth. It is important that we release, let go of negative codependent attachments, any attachments that keep us from growing. We are to love and care for all, but with an open hand. God is in control, not us, and it is our job to trust Him, to follow Him and to obey. The power of God's love heals us and sets us free. We are given new life and supernatural help through the Holy Spirit.

God delivers us from fear and heals us with His love.

We cannot compromise our new lives with any known sin, and we need to ask God to forgive and heal us of our self-deceptions. We also need to ask God for greater courage and guidance through His Holy Spirit. We need to trust that He is faithful to work in us. We are a work in process and are being purified to dwell in His presence forever. Pray this prayer. "Thank you, Lord Jesus, for your great love, for dying for my sins, and for giving me new life. Thank you for your peace, your unconditional love and compassion and for the knowledge of your will for my life. I give you praise and thanks and seek to glorify your name. Fill me with your Holy Spirit that I may do your Will, as I cannot manage my life on my own." Let us look to Jesus first in all areas of our lives. When people disappoint us, when life's worries weigh us down, we need to lay these aside and rest at Jesus' feet. He can fill the love needs we have. He can give the assurances that our needs will be met. He can give us the victory over disease, evil, and death. He can give us the supernatural power we need for victory. He can divinely inspire us to make the right choices, and to do what is right. He can comfort us, give us wisdom and understanding. He will protect us from spiritual harm. His power is great and mighty and He has already won the victory. He is our rock, our high place, our salvation. Thank you Lord. We love You and praise You.

Jesus looked on others with love and compassion. He wanted those in sin and darkness to see and hear His love. But many did not, because if they did, they would have to turn from their sins. Yet, it is in turning that we are healed. People cannot let fear of giving up sinful behaviors stand in the way of their freedom in Christ. We all need to surrender to Christ each day. We can labor for the Lord, be a Christian soldier, a warrior, be a minister of the gospel, and reflect God's great love. But that requires surrender, sacrifice, faith, perseverance and trust in God. Some will not heed His word or the call of the Holy Spirit and live a pure and righteous life. A follower of Christ gives up his life, lays it down, fights the fight, loses yet wins, and dies, yet never truly dies.

Our lives are hid in Christ. We walk in the resurrection power of the Holy Spirit. We bring some of heaven to earth by bearing witness of God's great love and power. He is our Heavenly Father. He commands that we love one another. "Perfect love hath no fear." We are to totally trust in Him to fill all our needs, to obey Him. He has promised to give us great joy, eternal life, peace, beauty, truth and freedom. He will wipe away all tears. In His presence is joy and love. There is no evil, no pain, disease, nor death in God's presence. He desires that we dwell with Him. Jesus has come to show us the way. His Holy Spirit has come to give us the power. Accept this into your heart today.

Jesus tells us to learn of Him. When studying the scriptures, we learn many things about Jesus. Jesus baptizes with the Holy Spirit. Our baptism in water is symbolic of a turning to Christ, a cleansing of the past sins, an affirmation of faith, a new life, a born again experience. To help us walk righteously in the newness of life, Jesus sends us His Holy Spirit to guide us and comfort us.

Jesus is the Son of God. He is a King who transcends time and space. He was able to perform miracles. He healed the sick, even from a distance. We can pray for healing for others who are far from us. He saves, not only the believer, but also His entire household. He forgives our sins. He tells us if we want to be well, we need to believe, have faith, rise up and take action.

Jesus has power over nature, disease, and death. He not only raises the dead; but also, he Himself rose from the dead. He has authority over mankind and power to execute judgment. He is one with God, His Father, who is Spirit. He tells us He and His Father will be one in Spirit with us. They will dwell with us in love.

Jesus came down from Heaven to lead a mortal life, yet because of who He is, He was able to overcome the world. He walked on water. He told us **not** to **doubt** nor be afraid but to have faith. When we read the words of Jesus, we are being infused with His Spirit, for he says His words are spirit and truth. They set us free.

God the Father must first draw someone to Jesus. God's spirit of love pulls us to Christ. We are forgiven and given new life. We become new creations in Christ. We are cleansed by the blood of the lamb. We are redeemed by love. We are then to walk in love and truth. Jesus is the light of the world. With His Holy Spirit in us, we can let our light shine and glorify God. Light dispels darkness.

As new creations in Christ, we abide in Jesus. He is our very lifeline. He gives us water that we never thirst. He sustains us and provides power. He gives us His peace, love and joy. He saves us, and we have eternal life in Him. Though we die a mortal death, we live an eternal life spiritually with

Him. If we believe in Him, we never die. We are to follow Jesus, to abide in Him, to keep His commandments, to serve others, to love unconditionally in His holiness, purity and truth. Satan, the ruler of evil and deception in this world, is already cast out of God's presence. People with hard hearts, blind eyes, refusing to turn to Jesus and repent, keep themselves separate from God's love and blessings and stay vulnerable to evil. Jesus tells us to abide in Him - in the light, and not have fellowship with the works of darkness.

Jesus is the way. He has prepared a place for us, an eternal habitation. He will receive us and remind us that He is always with us. His Holy Spirit, the Comforter, shows us the way.

Jesus reminds us to use His name, for there is power and authority in it. He tells us to ask in His name and we will receive. As we abide in Him and His home is with us, He gives us His peace and joy. We are to ask in His name, and we will receive. In Him we prosper and bear fruit. We grow spiritually into His likeness and become sanctified, ever more holy, pure and true. When we depart this earthly life, we go home to Him and all those who dwell in love. Let us prepare ourselves in sanctity, holiness, purity, and righteousness to dwell in His presence forever.

Jesus, My Higher Power

Jesus through His Holy Spirit Will Lead You through Your Life.

Jesus has told us the greatest commandment is to "Love one Another." This means, not only to love those who love us, but also to love those who hate us, or are angry or bitter towards us. He says, "Love your enemies." This love is without expectations nor conditions. Once we have known God's great love for us, His forgiveness of our sins, then we are better able to love and forgive others, even those who have hurt us deeply. The indwelling of His Holy Spirit helps us to do this. God sees the end from the beginning, the bigger picture. In His great mercy and love and in His sovereignty, He brings good out of disaster and love out of hate. In Him all things prosper, and we find victory over evil, sin, disease, and death. Jesus showed us that we can overcome. He did, and He wants us to know that we can too. He told us not to be afraid, not to doubt, but to believe and have faith. There is great, great power in this. Because we are so doubtful and lack the necessary faith, He told us to use His name, the name of Jesus, to access this power. This power is greater than any in this material world.

We pray that our Higher Power, Jesus, our Lord, Savior

and Redeemer, will reveal this power through His name and through His Holy Spirit. We thank Him for saving us and helping us overcome. We will dwell for eternity in His Presence - a place of extreme love, peace, beauty, joy and power. In this place, there is no pain. We will be healed, healthy, holy and whole. Thank you, Lord for this victory. Thank you for your love. We give you praise.

Rosemary is the co-author of *The Twelve Steps of Phobics Anonymous* and is a consultant and facilitator for Phobics Anonymous, a secular 12-step program. She is the founder of Phobics Victorious, a Christ-centered recovery program for suffering phobics and is the author of *One Day at a Time in Phobics Victorious* and *The Twelve Steps of Phobics Victorious*. She can be reached at:

56 Sunrise Drive, Rancho Mirage, CA 92270

Email: rosemaryjane@dc.rr.com

THE TWELVE STEPS

1. We admitted that we were powerless over people, places, and things, that our lives had become unmanageable.

2. Came to believe that a power greater than ourselves could restore us to wholeness.

3. Made a decision to turn our will and our lives over to the care of God, as we understood Him.

4. Made a searching, and fearless moral inventory of ourselves.

5. Admitted to God, to ourselves, and to another human being the exact nature of our wrongs.

6. Were entirely ready to have God remove all these defects of character.

7. Humbly asked Him to remove our shortcomings.

8. Made a list of all persons we had harmed, and became willing to make amends to them all.

9. Made direct amends to such people wherever possible, except when to do so would injure them or others.

10. Continued to take a personal inventory and when we were wrong promptly admitted it.

11. Sought through prayer and meditation to improve our conscious contact with God as we understood Him, praying only for knowledge of His will for us and the power to carry that out.

12. Having had a spiritual awakening as the result of these steps, we tried to carry this message to others and to practice these principles in all our affairs.

THE TWELVE TRADITIONS

1. Our common welfare should come first; personal recovery depends upon unity.

2. For our group purpose there is but one ultimate authority - a loving God as He may express Himself in our group conscience. Our leaders are but trusted servants, they do not govern.

3. The only requirement for membership is a desire to recover.

4. Each group should be autonomous except in matters affecting other groups as a whole.

5. Each group has but one primary purpose - to carry the message to those who still suffer.

6. A group ought never endorse, finance, or lend its name to any related facility or outside enterprise, lest problems of money, property or prestige divert us from our primary spiritual purpose.

7. Every group ought to be fully self-supporting, declining outside contributions.

8. Each group should remain forever nonprofessional, but our service centers may employ special workers.

9. Each group, as such, ought never be organized, but may create service boards or committees directly responsible to those they serve.

10. Each group has no opinion on outside issues; hence its name ought never be drawn into public controversy.

11. Our public relations policy is based on attraction rather than promotion; we need always maintain personal anonymity at the level of press, radio, and films.

12. Anonymity is the spiritual foundation of all our traditions, ever reminding us to place principles before personalities.

www.ingramcontent.com/pod-product-compliance
Lightning Source LLC
Chambersburg PA
CBHW030013040426
42337CB00012BA/762